First Published in the UK in 2013 by Focus Education (UK) Ltd.
Revised Sep 2014
Revised Sep 2015

Focus Education (UK) Ltd
Publishing
Talking Point Conference & Exhibition Centre
Huddersfield Road
Scouthead
Saddleworth
OL4 4AG

Focus Education (UK) Ltd. Reg. No 4507968

ISBN 978-1-909038-10-3

Companies, institutions and other organisations wishing to make bulk purchases of books published by
Focus Education should contact their local bookstore or Focus Education direct:
Customer Services, Focus Education, Talking Point Conference & Exhibition Centre,
Huddersfield Road, Scouthead, Saddleworth, OL4 4AG
Tel 01457 821818 Fax 01457 878205

www.focus-education.co.uk
customerservice@focus-education.co.uk
Printed in Great Britain by Focus Education UK Ltd

  Receive special offers, discounts & free samples of the latest publications!

About the author

Tim is a full time Consultant with Focus Education. This role involves leading large scale national conferences, working with groups of schools, working with individual schools and inspecting schools. Tim regularly mentors trainee inspectors.

Prior to joining Focus Education he worked as a head teacher. Tim's last school had a reputation for innovation and their initiatives have been utilised by others and presented internationally. He has a proven track record of impacting on school improvement. This has resulted in work as a local leader of education; a school improvement partner; an Ofsted inspector; and a professional partner.

Tim is experienced at working with teams in school with a focus on all core areas of school improvement, i.e. curriculum, assessment, teaching and learning, leadership and management, etc.

Tim is the author of a number of books, including most recently:

School Governors: A Guide to Effective Practice
Leading a Small School
Designing Pre and Post Learning Challenges
Religious Education Learning Challenge Curriculum
Mathematics Learning Challenge Curriculum
Preparing for Ofsted Inspection
Design and Technology Learning Challenge Curriculum
Enriching the Curriculum
Art and Design Learning Challenge Curriculum
Judging Teaching, not the Teacher
Judging EY Teaching, not the EY Teacher (with Sarah Quinn)

Prelude

"What stood out in these schools was the quality of leadership; the high expectations of staff and high aspirations for pupils"

Ofsted introduction to 'Twenty Outstanding Primary Schools – excelling against the odds'

"Jumping through hoops doesn't raise standards- ensuring students' everyday diet is of the highest quality does: that's what makes the difference."

Headteacher in response to recent inspection proposals

"You might not always get what you want, but you always get what you expect."

Charles Haddon Spurgeon, British priest

"High expectations are the key to everything"

Sam Walton, Founder of Wal-Mart

Contents

Section 1

Introduction

Introduction

As you may expect, many schools use the phrase 'high expectations' in their mission statement, prospectus, website and other similar material when describing outcomes for their pupils.

When asked to define what this means, the typical responses are:

"Ensuring every child fulfils his or her potential."

"Realising the talents of all."

"Treating every child as an individual and ensuring their needs are met in full."

"Everyone has the chance to shine."

Whilst not wishing to criticise any of these statements, all of which are worthy aims, the difficulty can be that one sentence is neither expansive enough to cover the wealth of provision and outcomes, nor specific enough to be truly meaningful and measurable.

Introduction

<u>Consistency</u>

Another common issue is that an agreed definition of 'high expectations' does not exist within a school. The head teacher may give one response, a deputy head teacher a different response and the chair of the governing body yet another differing response.

Introduction

The aim of this book is to enable school leaders to evidence high expectations in all aspects of their school's work.

This includes:

- The learning environment.
- Attainment and achievement.
- Pupil attitudes, values and behaviours.
- Pupil safety.

The book also examines the role of the subject leader in setting high expectations.

Introduction

Before reading any further, it may be useful to consider what your response would be if you were asked to define 'high expectations' in your context.

Would your answer differ if you were asked the same question by different people? For example, what if you were asked by a parent, a governor, a member of staff, a pupil or an inspector?

What would be the responses from your colleagues in the same situation?

The format overleaf can be used to sample the existing views of stakeholders. It could be given out at a staff meeting, governors' meeting or parents' evening.

What do we mean by 'high expectations' in our school?

Please list your thoughts below and return this form to the head teacher. Thank you.

High expectations means:

My role in school is_____

Introduction

The phrase 'high expectations' is often used in the School Inspection Handbook 2015, for example in the grade descriptors:

From the 'Quality of teaching in the school'

Outstanding   'Teachers have consistently **high expectations** of all pupils' attitudes to learning.

From 'The effectiveness of leadership and management'

Outstanding   'Leaders and governors have created a culture that enables pupils and staff to excel. They are committed unwaveringly to setting **high expectations** for the conduct of pupils and staff'

Good   'Leaders set **high expectations** of pupils and staff'

School inspection is an evidence based process. Inspectors will need to find strong evidence to support a judgement based on a school's 'high expectations' in both these areas.

Introduction

The Teachers' Standards also uses the phrase in the very first section. The bullet points offer some guidance as to what this looks like in practice:

A teacher must:

1 Set **high expectations** which inspire, motivate and challenge pupils

- establish a safe and stimulating environment for pupils, rooted in mutual respect
- set goals that stretch and challenge pupils of all backgrounds, abilities and dispositions
- demonstrate consistently the positive attitudes, values and behaviour which are expected of pupils.

Because of the importance of the Teachers' Standards in appraisal systems and pay progression it is vital that schools have a clear understanding of what these elements actually look like in their context.

Introduction

The three main sections of this book are therefore linked to the three bullet points in the first section of the Teachers' Standards.

Establish a safe and stimulating environment for pupils, rooted in mutual respect.

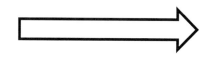

The Learning Environment
Pages 17 to 30

Set goals that stretch and challenge pupils of all backgrounds, abilities and dispositions.

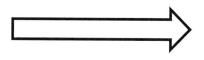

Setting Goals That Stretch And Challenge Pupils
Pages 31 to 56

Demonstrate consistently the positive attitudes, values and behaviour which are expected of pupils.

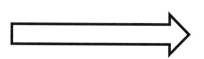

Attitudes, Values and Behaviour
Pages 57 to 65

Introduction

Activity One **What do we mean by a well educated young person?**

The core purpose of a school is, of course, to educate the pupils. Any activities within the school are therefore aimed at fulfilling this intention.

But to achieve this, the school needs to establish a consensus view of what the leadership team (including the governing body) and all of the staff mean by a 'well educated' young person.

The next page is a template for individuals to compile a list of what they believe constitutes a well-educated young person. The responses can then be collated and discussed to allow the school to arrive at a distilled view of the commonly agreed features.

Page 17 is a completed version that may be useful to provoke discussion and engage people in the activity.

A well-educated young person...

A well-educated young person...

IS AN INDEPENDENT LEARNER AND DECISION MAKER

is adaptable

has a sense of responsibility and discipline

has good relationships with adults and peers

IS MORALLY AND SPIRITUALLY AWARE

IS LITERATE AND A GOOD COMMUNICATOR

is able to operate as part of a team

uses numbers and ICT effectively

IS PREPARED FOR THE CHALLENGES OF SOCIETY

IS ADVENTUROUS AND WILLING TO TRY NEW THINGS

is tolerant and challenges stereotypes

cooperates as part of a team

HAS A SENSE OF WELL-BEING AND CAN LEAD A SAFE, FULFILLING LIFE

Activity One What do we mean by a 'well educated' young person?

Summary: In our school a well educated young person is one who:

Section 2

The Learning Environment

The Learning Environment

Remember, the Teachers' Standards state that, "A teacher must...establish a safe and stimulating environment for pupils."

It is worth considering what we mean by the 'learning environment'. Many definitions exist. One that neatly summarises the commonly occurring factors is that it can be described as:

'The sum of the internal and external circumstances and influences surrounding and affecting a person's learning.'

Mosby's Medical Dictionary, 8th edition.

Key Question

How does the environment of your school or setting affect your pupils?

The Learning Environment

<u>Activity Two</u> What is the school environment like for a pupil?

How often do staff ever look around the school from a pupil's perspective?

Why not take a tour of your school from a pupils' height and therefore from their viewpoint? This may mean kneeling or sitting down!

Another option is to film a tour of the school with the camera held at pupil eye level.

It would be very useful to begin where the pupils enter the school. What are the first things they notice? What message does this give the pupils? How is the school communicating that it has high expectations?

Repeat the process in hallways, cloakrooms, halls and classrooms.
A checklist is overleaf.

The Learning Environment

From a pupil's viewpoint:

- ❑ What is the first thing I will notice when I enter this part of the school? Is this 'positive' and linked to expectations and learning?

- ❑ Can I read the text on displays or is it too high up on the walls?

- ❑ Can I see the main whiteboard without leaning back too far?

- ❑ Can I actually see/read any work that is hanging from the ceiling?

- ❑ Can I reach the resources I need?

- ❑ Are there places the adults do not notice where there is damaged paintwork, graffiti or even anything that is unsafe?

The Learning Environment

The Online Environment

Many schools have spent a considerable amount of time and money developing a Virtual Learning Platform (VLP) or Virtual Learning Environment (VLE).

Other schools have links on their own website to relevant external websites such as BBC Learning.

The fundamental issue is the effect any form of online provision has on pupils' learning.

A couple of links to high quality external websites which are accessed by all the pupils will be far more effective than an activity that has taken a teacher a considerable amount of time to produce on the schools' VLP and is then only accessed by a few pupils.

The Learning Environment

A 'High Expectations' checklist for our school's online provision for learning.

✓ Is there consistency of approach? *(e.g. Do all parallel classes have similar experiences and access to online learning?)*

✓ Are resources relevant and up-to-date? *(e.g. Are online links pertinent to the theme the pupils are studying this term or this week?)*

✓ Are resources inviting and child friendly? *(e.g. Does the VLP engage pupils of all ages and can it be accessed by both younger and older pupils?)*

✓ Are online resources used to enhance learning and give pupils access to experiences that they can not experience in real life? *(e.g. the use of webcams to see aspects of life in other countries or satellite pictures of the weather in another part of the world. Compare this with the school that took pupils on a 'virtual tour' of a synagogue, when there was a real one just down the road.)*

The Learning Environment

A 'High Expectations' checklist for our school's online provision for learning.

✓ Does someone regularly check that links to activities are not 'broken'? *(e.g. pupils are not bringing in notes from parents saying that they could not access parts of the VLE or links to a website because of an error.)*

✓ Is your school's online environment consistent with the physical environment? *(e.g. Does it 'match' and give the same high quality messages about expectations and learning?)*

Finally, would you be as proud to show a visitor your online learning provision as you would to show them the actual school?

If not, why not? And what messages does this give pupils?

The Learning Environment

The Role of Subject Leaders

One aspect of the subject leader role is to monitor standards in their subject.

This normally involves activities such as the monitoring of teaching, checking planning and the scrutiny of pupils' work.

However, few subject leaders include monitoring of the learning environment (as it applies to their subject) in their work.

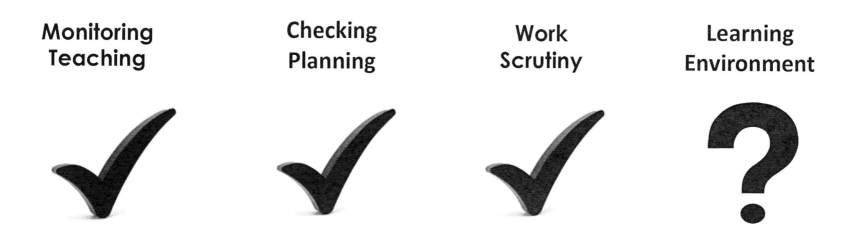

Monitoring Teaching   **Checking Planning**   **Work Scrutiny**   **Learning Environment**

The Learning Environment

The Role of Subject Leaders

A starting point may be to audit the school environment for factors which promote and benefit the particular subject and the factors that are potential barriers to learning or give negative messages about that subject. This immediately gives the subject leader examples of good practice to share with colleagues, thus ensuring consistency throughout the school, as well as areas for development.

An example from an audit for PE might look like this:

Positive aspects of the learning environment	Negative aspects of the learning environment
Extensive school fields, marked out as pitches for hockey and football. Rules for games on wall on Class Five facing the KS2 playground. Trophies won in local sports displayed in entrance (but rarely seen by pupils!)	Small playground area and line markings faded. No PE related display, except in one class. .

The Learning Environment

The Role of Subject Leaders

Learning environment audit for _____ Carried out by_____ Date____	
Positive aspects of the learning environment	**Negative aspects of the learning environment**

The Learning Environment

The Role of Subject Leaders

Subject leaders should ensure that their subject is perceived in a positive way by the pupils.

The high expectations they should be promoting in their subject should also be evident in the standard of work displayed around the school.

Key Question

Does the school's Display Policy concentrate only on the artistic qualities of display rather than the impact of display on learning?

Key Question

Do subject leaders ever monitor the standard of display in their subject?

The Learning Environment

The Role of Subject Leaders

Contrast these examples from two schools:

"Subject co-ordinators are often quietly pleased if they happen to see a display in a classroom or corridor linked to their subject. The Art Co-ordinator advises teachers and teaching assistants about the design and materials used and the emphasis is on the artistic merits of the finished display. Most pupils have at least one piece of work up somewhere in the school. Displays stay in place until they are replaced or become tatty."

"Subject leaders formally audit the quality of displayed work in their subject on a termly basis. Teachers have to be able to justify any display in terms of its impact on learning. Subject leaders can actually veto work from being displayed in the first place if the quality is not high enough, or it may lead to misconceptions in learning. All displays of pupils' work include the date they were put up and displays must be changed within a term unless specifically agreed with the subject leader."

The Learning Environment

The Role of Subject Leaders

Of the two examples on the previous page it is obvious which one best fits the Ofsted grade descriptor from the Quality of Leadership section which states,

"The pursuit of excellence in all of the school's activities is demonstrated by an uncompromising and highly successful drive..."

However, the majority of schools tend to better match the description of the first school rather than the second.

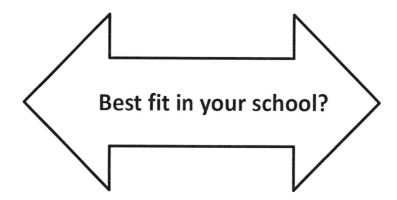

Best fit in your school?

The Learning Environment

Summary

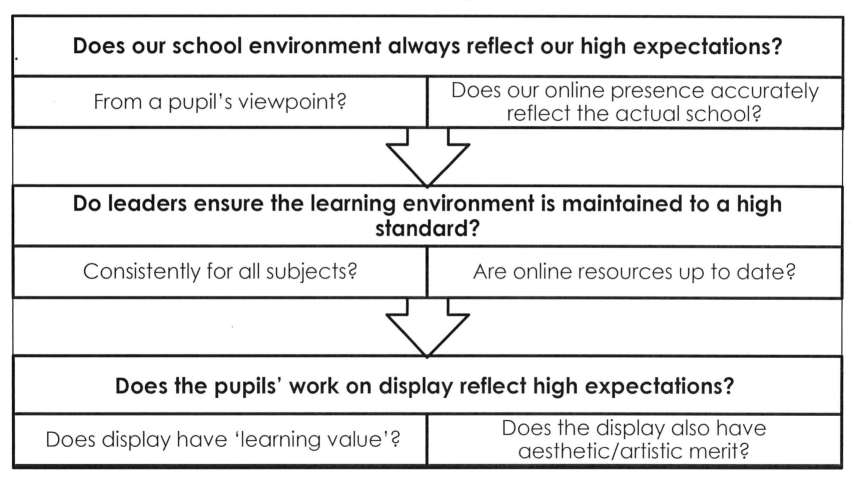

Does our school environment always reflect our high expectations?

| From a pupil's viewpoint? | Does our online presence accurately reflect the actual school? |

Do leaders ensure the learning environment is maintained to a high standard?

| Consistently for all subjects? | Are online resources up to date? |

Does the pupils' work on display reflect high expectations?

| Does display have 'learning value'? | Does the display also have aesthetic/artistic merit? |

The Learning Environment

Summary Statement

The school could agree a paragraph or list of bullet points to summarise this area, e.g.

In this school, our learning environment both reflects and enables the high expectations we have for our pupils.

Our learning environment:

Section 3

Setting Goals That Stretch
And Challenge Pupils

Setting Goals That Stretch And Challenge Pupils

Expected Progress

If goals or targets are going to challenge pupils, then the school leadership and the relevant staff must have an absolutely clear understanding of the following:

What are the starting points for our pupils? (Attainment on entry or AOE)

Progress

What level of attainment do our pupils reach when they leave?

The key issue is whether the progress between these two attainment points is good enough! This is the <u>achievement</u> of the pupils.

Some quotes from the Ofsted grade descriptors for Outcomes for Pupils are overleaf.

Setting Goals That Stretch And Challenge Pupils

From the 'Outcomes for pupils' grade descriptors,
School Inspection Handbook

Outstanding

'Throughout each year group and across the curriculum, including in English and mathematics, current pupils make substantial and sustained progress, developing excellent knowledge and understanding, considering their different starting points.'

'From each different starting point, the proportions of pupils making and exceeding expected progress in English and in mathematics are high compared with national figures. The progress of disadvantaged pupils matches or is improving towards that of other pupils nationally.'

Good

'Across almost all year groups and in a wide range of subjects, including in English and mathematics, current pupils make consistently strong progress, developing secure knowledge and understanding, considering their different starting points.

'From different starting points, the proportions of pupils making and exceeding expected progress in English and in mathematics are close to or above national figures. The progress of the vast majority of disadvantaged pupils is similar to or improving in relation to other pupils nationally.'

Setting Goals That Stretch And Challenge Pupils

Expected Progress

<u>Most Able Pupils</u>

It is worth considering how the needs of the most able pupils are being met in the school or academy.

Some settings have found it useful to discuss what this looks like in day to day practice across the curriculum and across all age groups.

Key Question

Can staff identify the most able pupils they teach
and describe how they are developing a depth of learning and mastery?

Setting Goals That Stretch And Challenge Pupils

Expected Progress

As national curriculum levels have been removed the emphasis is now very much on pupils achieving the end of key stage expectations for each subjects.

Schools are expected to have introduced tracking systems that enable them to rigorously analyse children's progress towards these expectations.

However, we are still in a period of transition with 2014/15 RAISE data being based on levels and used as one of the starting points for inspection.

The main points for schools to consider are that :

o The vast majority of pupils work within the expectations set out for their year group.

o Teachers have intimate knowledge of year group expectations for English (reading, writing and spoken English); mathematics and science.

Setting Goals That Stretch And Challenge Pupils

Expected Progress

o Settings maximise opportunities to apply English and mathematics skills across the wider curriculum.

o Schools and academies acknowledge that poverty is no excuse for under-achievement.

Pre-teaching

o A programme of pre-teaching may have to be designed aimed at closing the gap between old and new knowledge.

o The aim is to ensure that mid to lower attainers are ready to take on the objectives outlined in the new National Curriculum.

o There is an expectation that pupil premium grant funding may be used to support this programme.

Setting Goals That Stretch And Challenge Pupils

Of course, with the removal of National Curriculum levels inspectors will not have the same data to analyse. The School Inspection Handbook for use from September 2015 states:

'Ofsted will take a range of evidence into account when making judgements, including published performance data, the school's in-year performance information and work in pupils' books and folders. However, unnecessary or extensive collections of marked pupils' work are not required for inspection.'

'When considering the school's records for the progress of current pupils, inspectors will recognise that schools are at different points in their move towards adopting a system of assessment without national curriculum levels.'

Setting Goals That Stretch And Challenge Pupils

The School Inspection Handbook then clarifies how inspectors will reach a judgement on outcomes. It states,

'In judging achievement, inspectors will give most weight to pupils' progress. They will take account of pupils' starting points in terms of their prior attainment and age when evaluating progress. Within this, they will give most weight to the progress of pupils currently in the school, taking account of how this compares with the progress of recent cohorts, where relevant. Inspectors will consider the progress of pupils in all year groups, not just those who have taken or are about to take examinations or national tests. As part of pupils' progress, inspectors will consider the growth in pupils' security, breadth and depth of knowledge, understanding and skills.'

Key Question

Are children in all cohorts on track to meet their end of year expectations, and therefore their end of key stage expectations and how do teachers and leaders track this?

Setting Goals That Stretch And Challenge Pupils

Expected Progress

So rather than systems of expected progress being based on sub-levels per year or points progress per term, schools will have their own systems based on the end of key stage expectations and age related expectations.

With the introduction of standardised Reception baselines, schools will be able to show how they have 'added value' by increasing the percentage of each cohort who meet age expectations as the cohort moves up through the school.

Another area to consider is the percentage of pupils who are able to work at mastery level. A school with high expectations will have staff who can plan for this and give pupils opportunities to develop a depth of learning and the ability to apply skills and knowledge across a range of subjects.

.

Setting Goals That Stretch And Challenge Pupils

The Role of Subject Leaders

Subject leaders should be aware of what constitutes appropriate challenge for pupils of all ages and abilities in the school.

It therefore stands to reason that they should know the starting points for the pupils, including the areas of the EYs curriculum relevant to their subject.

> ### Key Question
> Can a subject leader discuss and explain starting points relevant to their subject on entry to the school or setting?

The format overleaf is a simple way of plotting the number (or percentage) of pupils correlated against age related expectations in that subject at the end of key stages. As well as attainment on entry, Year 4 is included as a mid-way check through Key Stage Two.

Setting Goals That Stretch And Challenge Pupils

The Role of Subject Leaders

Subject_____ Date_____ Competed by_____

Well above					
Above					
In line					
Below					
Well below					
	AoE	Out Rec	Out Y2	Out Y4	Out Y6

Setting Goals That Stretch And Challenge Pupils

Summary

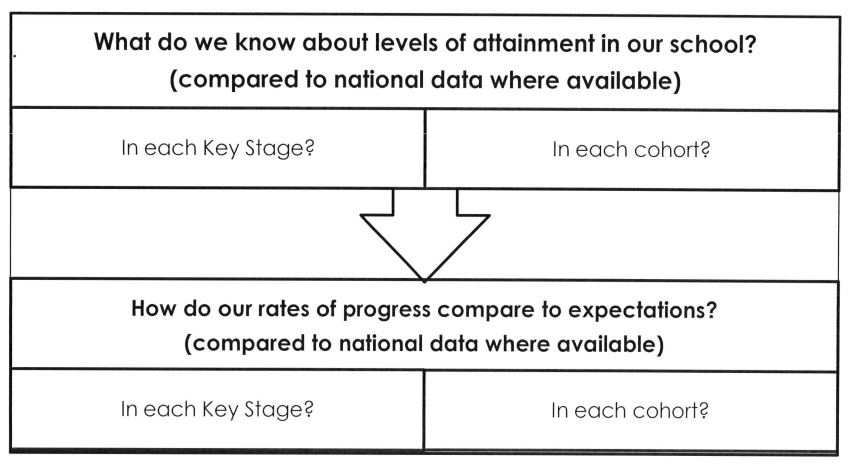

What do we know about levels of attainment in our school?
(compared to national data where available)

In each Key Stage?	In each cohort?

How do our rates of progress compare to expectations?
(compared to national data where available)

In each Key Stage?	In each cohort?

Setting Goals That Stretch And Challenge Pupils

Summary Statement

The school could agree a paragraph or list of bullet points to summarise this area e.g.

In this school, we have high expectations for our pupils.

Through target setting and ensuring challenge for the pupils we:

Section 4

Attitudes, Values and Behaviour

Attitudes, Values and Behaviour

Pupils' attitudes are referred to in the Ofsted grade descriptors for 'Personal development, behaviour and welfare.'

<u>Outstanding</u>   'Pupils are confident, self-assured learners. Their excellent **attitudes** to learning have a strong, positive impact on their progress.'

<u>Good</u>   'Pupils' **attitudes** to all aspects of their learning are consistently positive. These positive **attitudes** have a good impact on the progress they make.'

<u>Inadequate</u>   'Pupils show negative **attitudes** about the value of good manners and behaviour as key factors in school life, adult life and work.'

Attitudes, Values and Behaviour

Activity Three **Are our pupils learning?**

On the next learning walk or similar monitoring exercise undertaken by leaders in the school, focus on what the pupils are actually doing in lessons.

Are they involved in their learning? If so, how do you know?

Or are they disengaged? Again, how do you know? Is a child really concentrating, considering a response, formulating an idea or just day-dreaming?

This focus during fairly informal monitoring could develop into systems for evaluating and reporting through more formal monitoring procedures.

The key element is the *impact* any activity is having on learning. And a key way of evaluating this impact is in discussion with the children themselves.

Attitudes, Values and Behaviour

Pupil Safety

Schools work extremely hard to ensure their pupils stay safe and that they learn safe practices.

Safeguarding and child protection policies and practice are obviously a high priority.

Typically, schools arrange visits from the police, fire service and other organisations to work with the pupils so they learn about keeping themselves safe in a range of situations. The curriculum normally includes opportunities to learn about what constitutes safe and unsafe situations.

It may be worth checking how well the school's provision in this area meets the criterion of 'High Expectations'.

Attitudes, Values and Behaviour

Pupil Safety Checklist

❑ Pupils say they feel safe in and around the school. Their responses are checked on a regular basis.

❑ The effectiveness of outside providers and visitors is reviewed and altered to ensure maximum impact on pupil outcomes.

❑ All staff are made aware of relevant policies and practices during their induction.

❑ Pupils learn about any potentially dangerous locations near the school e.g. railway lines, electricity sub-stations, waterways, building sites etc.

❑ Pupils are fully involved in safe practice (see example on overleaf)

Attitudes, Values and Behaviour

Pupil Safety

An example of exemplary practice:

In every class from Reception to Year 6 pupils were involved in the risk assessment process. During morning registration a pair of pupils on a rota would complete a laminated risk assessment sheet for their own class. In Reception classes this was a set of six photographs: the outdoor area clean and tidy; the cloakroom with all the coats hung up so there was nothing to trip over; the sink area with the floor dry; the gate to the entrance locked; outside on a really hot day and outside on an icy day. The risk assessment was then placed on a display stand next to the whiteboard and discussed as necessary. If any were not ticked then the class knew not to go there until it had been rectified by an adult. The last two informed the children what to wear outside (sun hats or scarfs and hats). The format for older pupils was text based but the process was the same.

The risk assessment pro forma for all trips and visits included a section for 'Pupils' Views'. The teacher leading a trip or visit would discuss the destination and means of transport with all the pupils involved at an age appropriate level. Any relevant issues the pupils raised could be added to the risk assessment.

Attitudes, Values and Behaviour

Summary

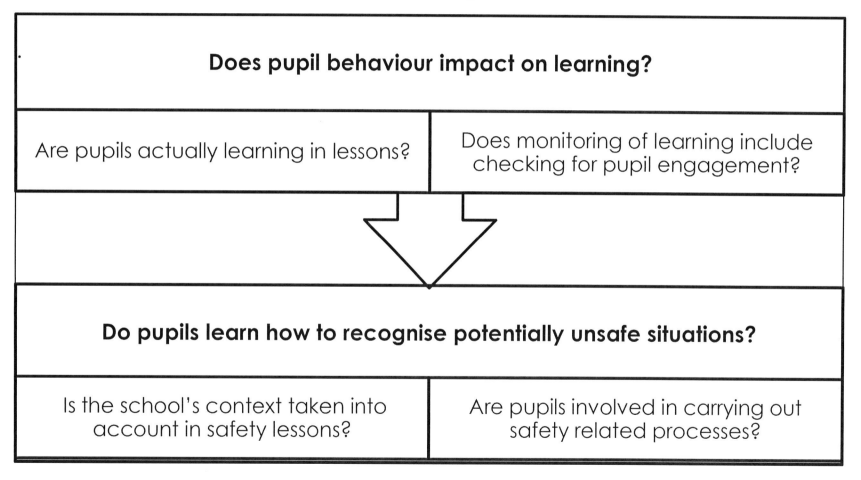

Does pupil behaviour impact on learning?

Are pupils actually learning in lessons?	Does monitoring of learning include checking for pupil engagement?

Do pupils learn how to recognise potentially unsafe situations?

Is the school's context taken into account in safety lessons?	Are pupils involved in carrying out safety related processes?

Attitudes, Values and Behaviour

Summary Statement

The school could agree a paragraph or list of bullet points to summarise this area e.g.

In this school, our pupils attitudes, values and behaviour reflect our high expectations and this impacts positively on their learning.

This is demonstrated by:

Section 5

Summary

Summary

The school may find it useful to draw together their thoughts to produce a summary statement defining 'High Expectations' in their setting.

This could be produced by the governing body and leadership team.

It could be useful to then include this information in induction materials for new staff and governors. It could also be available for other stakeholders, perhaps via the school website.

A suggested template is given overleaf.

Summary

In our school we have high expectations for all our pupils.

This is so they can become well educated young people with the following qualities: *(see Activity One on page 13)*

The learning environment includes all areas of the school itself as well as our website/virtual learning platform. This both reflects and promotes our high expectations by: (see summary on page 31)

The learning goals we set our pupils and the consistent level of challenge in all lessons will be effected by: (see summary on page 52)

We will instil attitudes, values and behaviours in all our pupils that will impact in a positive way on their learning by: (see summary on page 61)